I Made It Myself!

Art Foam Fun

Hélène Leroux-Hugon

GARETH STEVENS
GS
PUBLISHING
A Member of the WRC Media Family of Companies

The author and publishers thank Amandine for the photographs.

Please visit our web site at: www.garethstevens.com
For a free color catalog describing Gareth Stevens Publishing's
list of high-quality books and multimedia programs, call
1-800-542-2595 (USA) or 1-800-387-3178 (Canada).
Gareth Stevens Publishing's fax: (414) 332-3567.

Library of Congress Cataloging-in-Publication Data

Leroux-Hugon, Hélène.
    [Douces mousses. English]
    Art foam fun / Hélène Leroux-Hugon.
        p. cm. — (I made it myself!)
    ISBN 0-8368-5964-2 (lib. bdg.)
    1. Plastics craft. 2. Plastic foams. 3. Foam materials.
I. Title. II. Series.
TT297.L45 2005
    745.57'2—dc22   2005046501

This edition first published in 2006 by
Gareth Stevens Publishing
A Member of the WRC Media Family of Companies
330 West Olive Street, Suite 100
Milwaukee, Wisconsin 53212 USA

This U.S. edition copyright © 2006 by Gareth Stevens, Inc.
Original edition first published by Larousse-Bordas, Paris,
France, under the title *Tout en mousse: Douces Mousses*,
copyright © Dessain et Tolra / Larousse, Paris 2004.

Photography: Cactus Studio
Translation: Muriel Castille
English text: Dorothy L. Gibbs
Gareth Stevens series editor: Dorothy L. Gibbs
Gareth Stevens art direction and cover design: Tammy West
Gareth Stevens graphic design: Jenni Gaylord

Printed in the United States of America

1 2 3 4 5 6 7 8 9 09 08 07 06 05

CONTENTS

Page 4   **Helpful Hints**

Page 6   **Frog-Face Mask**

Page 8   **Butterfly Crown**

Page 10   **Stylish Bracelets**

Page 12   **Pencil Pot**

Page 14   **Pencil Pals**

Page 16   **Party Picks**

Page 18   **Piggy Mask**

Page 20   **Napkin Rings**

Page 22   **Patterns**

Helpful Hints

Soft, flexible art foam, also called craft foam, can be found in craft and art supply stores as well as in some hobby shops. It comes in both sheets and shapes. All of the projects in this book use sheets of art foam (one project also uses a medium-size foam ball). Foam sheets are easy to cut, glue, and bend, and they come in many bright colors. Most foam sheets are about $\frac{1}{16}$ inch (2 millimeters) thick. Thicker sheets are about $\frac{1}{8}$ inch (3 mm).

GLUING

The kind of glue you use on art foam is important. Glues with solvents or other harsh chemicals can damage the foam. Always use a nontoxic, water-based craft glue for your art foam projects. You can find the right kinds of glue in the same craft and art supply stores that sell art foam sheets and shapes. The instructions for the projects in this book tell you to use thick foam sheets for the parts on which you will glue other pieces. The additional thickness provides good support for the finished project. Thinner sheets are fine to use for the shapes you will be gluing on top of your support pieces. When you are finished with a project, it is a good idea to put it under or inside of a heavy book, for a while, to help make sure that all the pieces hold together well.

4

CUTTING

Before you cut any art foam, you might want to practice a little on sheets of heavy construction paper. Cut some straight lines, then practice some curved lines and circles of different sizes. When you feel comfortable cutting construction paper, you'll be ready to start drawing shapes directly on foam sheets and cutting them out.

TRACING AND TRANSFERRING

For the projects in this book that have patterns to transfer onto sheets of art foam, you will first have to trace the patterns onto paper. You will need thin white paper, or specially made tracing paper, and a pencil with soft lead. Lay the paper over the pattern you want to trace. You will be able to see the pattern through the paper. Use your pencil to draw the pattern on the paper, following the lines of the pattern that you can see through the paper. To transfer the pattern onto a sheet of foam, turn the paper over and, using the side of the lead in your pencil, rub color over the whole back side of your drawing. Then, just lay the paper, colored side down, on a sheet of foam and draw over the pattern with your pencil.

5

Frog-Face Mask

If you could be any animal, wouldn't you want to be a green-spotted blue frog? When you wear this mask, don't be surprised if you feel like hopping around!

Materials:
- thick sheet of blue art foam
- thin sheets of white, black, and green art foam
- scissors
- glue
- hole punch
- black elastic thread*

*The elastic thread should be just long enough to fit around the back of your head, from the front of one ear to the front of the other ear.

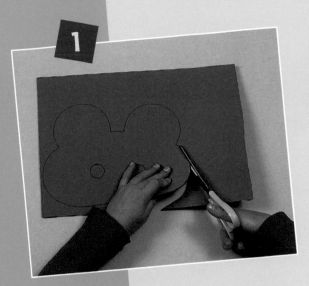

1

Trace the frog mask pattern on page 22 and transfer it onto a thick sheet of blue art foam. Cut out the foam shape, which is the frog's head.

2

Trace the large circle patterns on page 22 and transfer them onto a thin sheet of white art foam. Trace the small circle patterns on page 22 and transfer them onto a thin sheet of black art foam. Cut out all of the white and black circles. Glue the white circles (the eyes) in place at the top of the mask, then glue the black circles (the pupils) on top of the white circles.

3

Hold the mask up to your face. Have a grown-up mark where the eyeholes should be and cut out the eyeholes, making them about the same size as the frog's pupils. Cut about 25 small spots, in different sizes and irregular shapes, out of thin green art foam. Glue the spots all over the front of the mask. Punch a hole on each side of the mask, straight out from the eyeholes. Put one end of the elastic thread in each hole and knot it.

Butterfly Crown

This beautiful butterfly crown is fit for a queen, and it's as easy as 1-2-3! Add colorful art foam circles to look like jewels in your crown.

Materials:
- thick sheets of black and blue art foam
- thin sheet of white art foam
- scraps of thin art foam in several bright colors
- pinking scissors*
- scissors
- glue
- stapler

*Pinking scissors have saw-toothed blades that leave a zigzag edge when they cut.

Cut a wide strip of thick black art foam. Use pinking scissors to give the foam strip a decorative edge. The strip should be long enough to reach around your head with the ends overlapping a little bit.

Trace the butterfly wings pattern on page 23 and transfer it onto a thick sheet of blue art foam. Cut out the shape and glue it to the center of the black foam strip.

Trace the butterfly body pattern on page 23 and transfer it onto a thin sheet of white art foam. Cut out the shape and glue it to the center of the wings. Cut strips of black foam and glue them across the body. Cut circles of different sizes and colors out of scraps of thin art foam and glue them onto the wings in a design you like. Ask a grown-up to help you fit the black strip of foam to your head size and staple the ends together.

9

Stylish Bracelets

Make colorful — and comfortable — bracelets by cutting soft art foam into simple shapes and gluing the shapes onto foam bands in designs that you create yourself. These stylish, foam fashion accessories are not only soft but also light as a feather.

Materials:
- thick sheets of purple and yellow art foam
- scraps of thin green art foam and several other bright colors
- scissors
- pinking scissors
- glue
- stapler

1

Cut a strip of thick purple art foam that is 1½ inches (4 centimeters) wide and about 9 inches (23 cm) long. Then, cut a strip of thick yellow art foam the same size.

2

Cut one or two long, narrow strips of thin green art foam. Use pinking scissors to give the strips a zigzag edge. Then use regular scissors to cut the thin green strip (or strips) into short pieces. Each piece should be 1½ inches (4 cm) long. Glue the short pieces of green foam onto the wide purple strip, spacing them equal distances apart.

3

Cut scraps of thin art foam into small circles, ovals, or other shapes you like. Use several different colors of foam to make the shapes decorative. Glue the shapes all over one side of the wide yellow strip of art foam. One at a time, fit the purple and yellow strips loosely around your wrist. (You must be able to easily slip each bracelet on and off over your hand.) Overlap the ends of each strip and staple them together.

Pencil Pot

Art foam can turn an empty tin can into an attractive and useful pot for storing your pencils, pens, paintbrushes, and colored markers. Be sure that the can you use is clean and dry and has no sharp edges.

Materials:
- thick sheet of yellow art foam
- thin sheet of black art foam
- empty tin can (thoroughly cleaned and the label removed)
- scissors
- glue
- strong tape

Have a grown-up help you measure around the outside of an empty tin can. Cut a rectangle of thick yellow art foam that is slightly longer than the outside measurement of the can and slightly wider than the height of the can.

Cut shapes such as dots, spots, and blobs out of a thin sheet of black art foam. You could try to make your shapes look like the spots on a giraffe. Glue the shapes all over one side of the yellow rectangle. After all the shapes are glued on, put the yellow rectangle inside or under a heavy book, for a while, to help the shapes stick tightly in place.

Spread glue all over the outside of the tin can and wrap the black-spotted piece of yellow art foam around the can. Use strong tape to hold down the overlapping end of the yellow foam until the glue dries completely and the foam is sticking tightly to the can.

Pencil Pals

Putting a cat, a mouse, a king, or a Martian at the end of your pencil can make writing and drawing a lot more fun! Write your own stories for a puppet show and let your pencils perform them. After making a cat pencil pal, you'll be ready to try all kinds of kooky characters.

Materials:
- scraps of thin red and black art foam
- medium-size purple foam ball
- scissors
- glue
- small moveable eyes

Cut a small, round nose out of a scrap of thin red art foam. Cut fringelike whiskers and two small triangles (the cat's ears) out of a scrap of black art foam. Place the purple ball in front of you. Glue the nose on the front of the ball, in the center. Then glue the ears onto the top of the ball.

Glue two moveable eyes onto the front of the ball between the nose and the ears. Glue the whiskers on each side of the red nose.

After you finish the cat's face, ask a grown-up to cut a deep X into the bottom of the cat's head. Now just stick a pencil into the X cut and start writing or drawing!

15

Party Picks

Having a party? Why not dress up some wooden toothpicks for the occasion? You can use your pretty party picks to decorate foods for meals or snacks, too. Just stick the picks into pastries, meatballs, sandwiches, or pieces of fruit. Start with a simple heart design, then follow the same basic steps to create a variety of colorful toothpick toppers.

Materials:
- thick sheets of black and green art foam
- thin sheet of red art foam
- scissors
- pinking scissors
- glue
- wooden toothpick

1

Cut a rectangle, about 2 inches (5 cm) long and 1½ inches (4 cm) wide, out of thick black art foam. Use pinking scissors to cut a smaller rectangle out of green art foam.

2

Glue the two rectangles together and stick a wooden toothpick in between them.

3

Cut a small heart shape out of thin red art foam. Glue it onto the green rectangle. A sun, a moon, a star, and a flower are some other shapes that are easy to make, but don't be afraid to try some fancier designs, too.

Piggy Mask

If you don't want your friends to recognize you, this pink pig mask is a perfect disguise. It is particularly perfect with pigtails — but watch out for a wolf when you wear it!

Materials:
- thick sheet of pink art foam
- thin sheet of red art foam
- scissors
- glue
- hole punch
- black elastic thread*

*The elastic thread should be just long enough to fit around the back of your head, from the front of one ear to the front of the other ear.

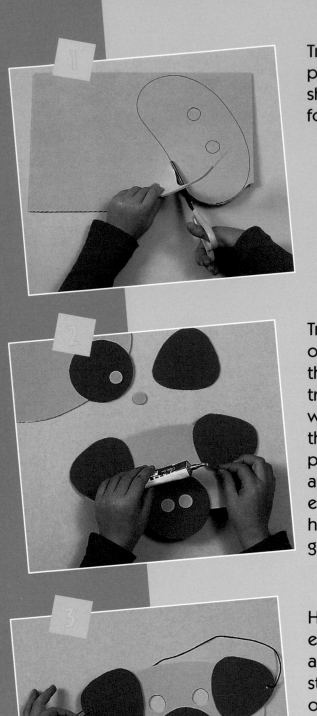

Trace the pig mask pattern on page 24 and transfer it onto a thick sheet of pink art foam. Cut out the foam shape, which is the pig's head.

Trace the pig nose and pig ear patterns on page 24 and transfer them onto a thin sheet of red art foam. (Be sure to transfer the pig ear pattern twice so you will have two ears for your mask.) Trace the two small circles on the pig nose pattern and transfer them onto pink art foam. Cut out the red nose and ears and glue them in place on the pig's head. Cut out the two pink circles and glue them in place on the red nose.

Have a grown-up help you cut the eyeholes out of your pig mask. Punch a hole at the outer edge of each ear, straight out from each eyehole. Put one end of the elastic thread through each hole and tie a knot in the thread to hold it in place.

19

Napkin Rings

Cleverly decorated foam rings will keep your napkins looking neat, but they will also help identify everyone's place at the dinner table. Let your mom, dad, brothers, and sisters each pick their favorite colors, but you can surprise them with your designs. Make this ladybug your first design, then try a fish on your own.

Materials:
- thick sheet of green art foam
- thin sheets of black and red art foam
- scissors
- pinking scissors
- glue
- stapler

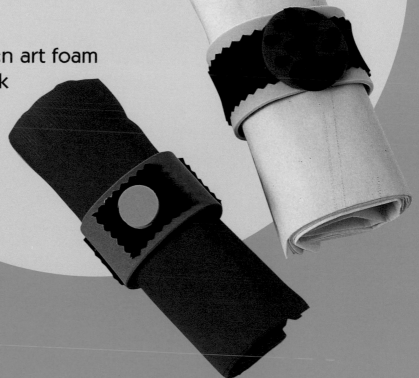

Cut a strip of thick green art foam that is 8 inches (20 cm) long and 1½ inches (4 cm) wide.

Cut a strip of thin black art foam that is 8 inches (20 cm) long and 1 inch (2½ cm) wide. Use pinking scissors to cut the black strip so it will have decorative, zigzag edges. Glue the black strip onto the green strip.

Cut a circle, about 1½ inches (4 cm) across, out of red art foam (for the ladybug's body). Using scraps of black art foam, cut out a small, round circle (the head), a thin black strip, and lots of little spots. Glue all of the black pieces in place on the red circle, then glue the finished ladybug to the center of the black strip. Staple the ends of the strip together to form a ring. Add a rolled-up napkin — and you're done!

21

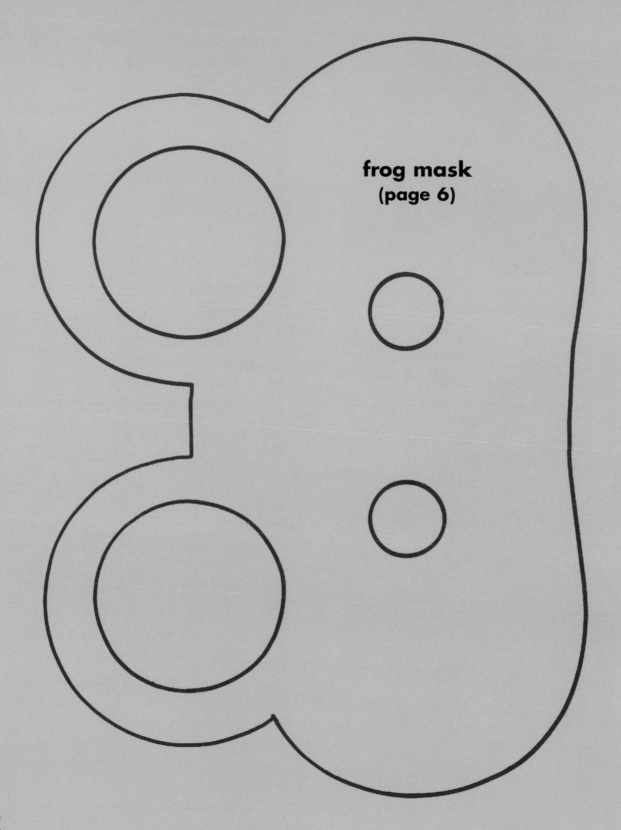

frog mask
(page 6)

22

butterfly wings
(page 8)

butterfly body
(page 8)

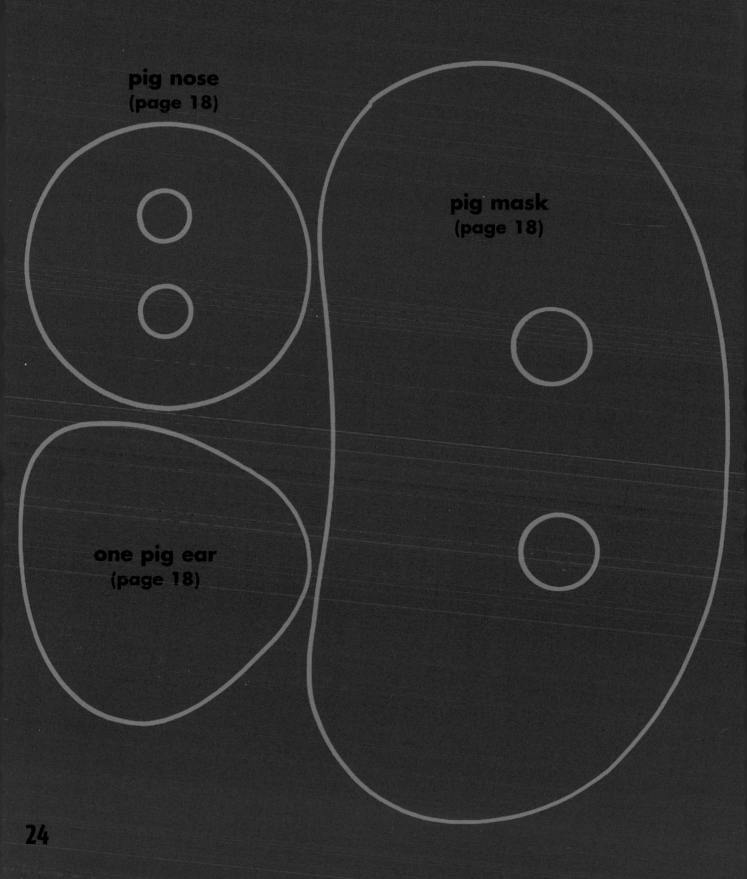

pig nose
(page 18)

pig mask
(page 18)

one pig ear
(page 18)

24